BAKE IT
AND
BUILD IT

Written by Elizabeth MacLeod

Illustrated by Tracy Walker

KIDS CAN PRESS

For Mary Beth,
who inspired many of these crafts — E.M.

Text copyright © 1998 by Elizabeth MacLeod
Illustrations copyright © 1998 by Tracy Walker

KIDS CAN DO IT and the logo are trademarks of Kids Can Press Ltd.

Published in Canada by
Kids Can Press Ltd.
29 Birch Avenue
Toronto, ON M4V 1E2

Published in the U.S. by
Kids Can Press Ltd.
85 River Rock Drive, Suite 202
Buffalo, NY 14207

Edited by Valerie Wyatt and Laura Ellis
Designed by Karen Powers
Food Styling by Pat Stephens
Photography by Frank Baldassarra
Printed in Hong Kong by Wing King Tong Co. Ltd.

CM 98 0 9 8 7 6 5 4 3 2 1

Canadian Cataloguing in Publication Data

MacLeod, Elizabeth
Bake it and build it

(Kids Can do it)
ISBN 1-55074-427-5

1. Bread dough craft — Juvenile literature. 2. Cookies — Juvenile literature.
I. Walker, Tracy. II. Title.

TT880.M353 1998   j745.5   C98-930468-X

Contents

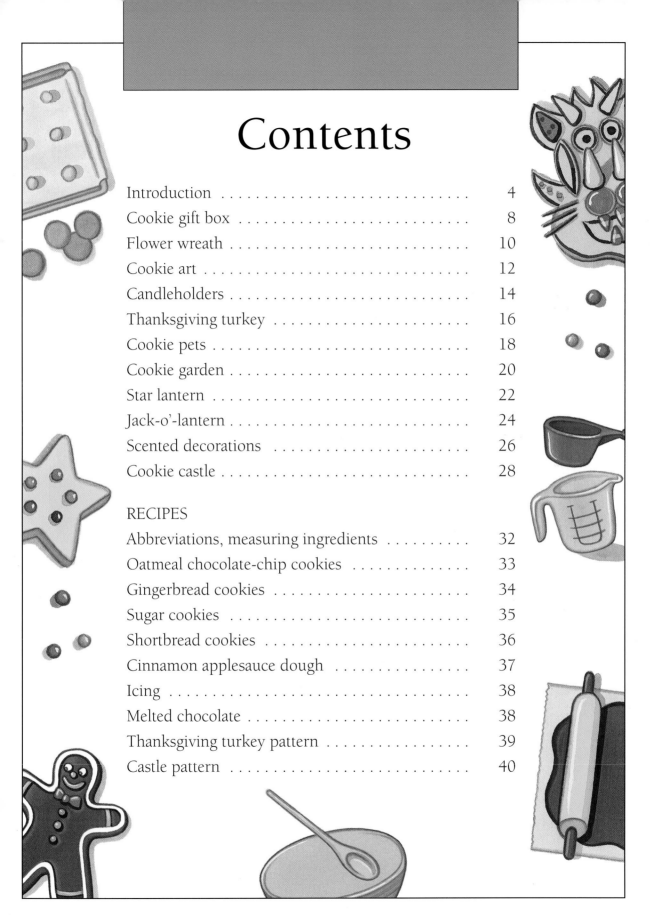

Introduction

You may have crafted with cardboard or printed with paints, but have you ever created with cookies? It's fun and easy, and the best part is you can eat your mistakes!

The word cookie comes from the Dutch word koekje, which means "little cake." Most cookies are flat and round like small cakes, but they can be baked in just about any shape. In this book you'll find out how to turn cookies into castles, candleholders and even cards. Once you've made the projects in this book, let your imagination go wild and cook up your own cookie creations.

COOKIE RECIPES

Each of the projects is made from cookie dough. To make the dough, follow the easy recipes at the back of the book.

BAKING SHEETS

Baking sheets should be flat. If they are bent or warped, the cookies may turn out curved instead of flat, making them difficult to attach to other cookies. You'll find it faster and easier to make many of the projects in this book if you use several baking sheets. It's also a good idea to use baking sheets lined with aluminum foil. The foil makes the cookies easy to remove, and the shiny surface helps the cookies bake properly. You can reuse the foil if you wipe it off well.

OVEN SAFETY

Use a thick pair of oven mitts to handle hot baking sheets. Ask an adult to help you when moving baking sheets in or out of the oven.

ROLLING OUT DOUGH

Big pieces of cookie dough can often be rolled out right on a baking sheet. Just lightly dust the rolling pin with flour to keep it from sticking to the dough.

To roll out smaller pieces of dough, you'll need waxed paper, a rolling pin and some all-purpose flour. Put a large piece of waxed paper on a table or countertop. A dab of water under each corner will hold the paper in place. Sprinkle a little flour on the waxed paper and on the rolling pin. Place the cookie dough on the waxed paper, roll it out to the thickness you want, cut out the cookies and place them on a baking sheet. Combine any leftover dough scraps, roll again and repeat until you've used all the dough. Or store leftover dough in waxed paper in the fridge.

ENLARGING PATTERN PIECES

Some of the projects are made from the patterns on pages 39 to 40. You can enlarge these patterns on a photocopier. Or you can use the grid the patterns are printed on to enlarge them. The lines of the grid are all 1.25 cm (½ in.) apart. So to make your pattern twice as big, on a piece of paper rule out a grid with lines that are 2.5 cm (1 in.) apart. Then copy what you see in each box of the small grid onto the larger grid.

Always ask an adult to help you when moving baking sheets in and out of the oven or when handling and cutting hot cookies.

BAKING YOUR COOKIES

When placing cookies on baking sheets, leave lots of room between cookies. (The cookies may expand as they bake.) Set one baking sheet at a time in the middle of a preheated oven. Cookies bake more evenly if there is only one baking sheet in the oven at a time.

COOKING TIMES

Cooking times vary from oven to oven. Bake your cookies for the minimum time suggested, then test them to see if they're done. They are done when the dough is no longer soft and the color has changed. You may want to set a timer to remind you to keep checking them.

GLUING PIECES TOGETHER

Wait until cookie pieces are completely cool before attaching them together. For cookies that have chocolate chips in them, or that you want to decorate with chocolate, use melted chocolate (page 38) as glue. For other cookies, use icing (page 38). Pour icing or slightly cooled melted chocolate into a small, heavy plastic bag, such as a freezer bag. When the bag is partly filled, snip off a tiny piece of one bottom corner.

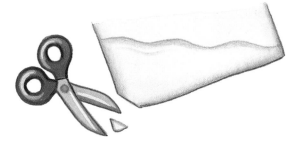

Twist the bag closed and hold it firmly shut so that the contents don't come out the top as you work. Squeeze the bag until some chocolate or icing comes out. This is called "piping." Cut the hole bigger if you want more chocolate or icing to come out.

For projects that you won't be eating, you can use white glue instead of chocolate or icing. When giving a project as a gift, make sure to tell the person if white glue has been used on it.

DECORATING YOUR COOKIES

You can find candy, sprinkles, colored sugar and tinted icing for decorating your cookies at grocery stores, bulk-food stores or cake-decorating stores. Choose candies with bright, strong colors. Light-colored candies look best on dark cookies and dark candies look good on light-colored cookies. Besides candies, try decorating with pretzels, taco chips or cereal.

REPAIRING YOUR COOKIES

If a cookie breaks, glue it back together with icing or melted chocolate (page 38). As long as you won't be eating the project, you can also break toothpicks in half and push them through the broken pieces to hold them together. Be sure to let a glued-together piece harden completely before you handle it again.

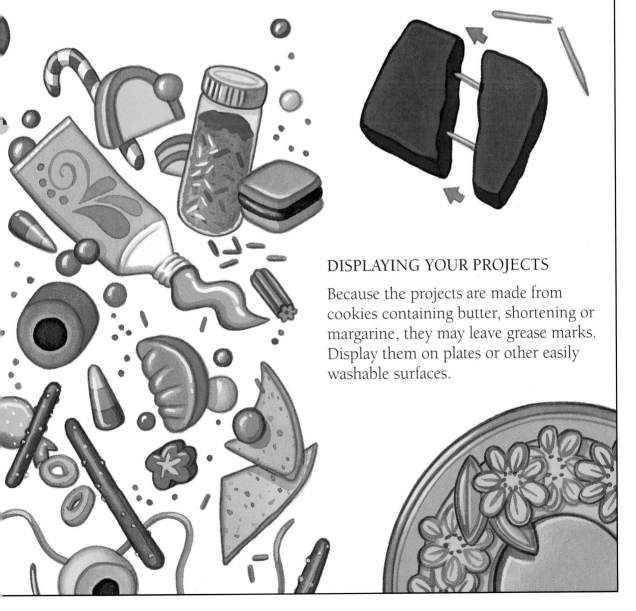

DISPLAYING YOUR PROJECTS

Because the projects are made from cookies containing butter, shortening or margarine, they may leave grease marks. Display them on plates or other easily washable surfaces.

Cookie gift box

Fill this very special box with cookies, chocolates, small gifts — or the recipe for the cookie dough.

YOU WILL NEED

- 1 recipe of oatmeal chocolate-chip cookie dough (page 33)
- 50 mL (¼ c.) melted chocolate (page 38)
- cookie decorations, including icing (page 38)

UTENSILS

a baking sheet lined with aluminum foil, a rolling pin, a ruler, a table knife, a lifter, a cooling rack, waxed paper, 4 large cans of food for supports

1 Preheat the oven to 180°C (350°F).

2 Place the dough on the baking sheet, then pat it and roll it out with the rolling pin until it is a little more than 0.5 cm (¼ in.) thick.

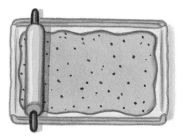

3 Use the ruler and the table knife to cut out the sides of the box from the dough. You'll need one square 9 cm x 9 cm (3 ½ in. x 3 ½ in.) for the top of the box and five squares 7.5 cm x 7.5 cm (3 in. x 3 in.) for the bottom and sides. Remove all extra dough and use it to make another box or cookies.

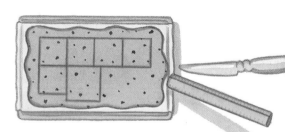

4 Bake the box pieces for 10 to 12 minutes. Remove from the oven and let cool on the baking sheet for 5 minutes. Use the lifter to transfer the pieces to the cooling rack.

5 When the pieces are cool, place a piece of waxed paper on a table and set one of the squares on it. This will be the bottom of the box.

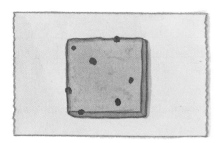

6 Using the table knife, spread melted chocolate on one edge of the bottom piece. Then spread melted chocolate along one edge of a side piece as shown and press the two chocolate-covered edges together. Support the side with a can. Repeat for the opposite side.

7 Spread melted chocolate along the vertical edges of the side pieces. Fit the remaining two sides in place and support them with the other two cans. Let stand until the chocolate hardens.

8 Fill the box. If you are putting something non-edible inside, wrap it in plastic, foil or waxed paper first. Place the top on the box. If you like, tie up the box with shoestring licorice and add a gift tag made from fruit leather. Or use melted chocolate or icing to glue other decorations onto your box.

Flower wreath

*This wreath makes a great
Mother's Day or Valentine's Day gift.*

YOU WILL NEED

- 1 recipe of sugar cookie dough (page 35)
- 1 recipe of icing (page 38)
- cookie decorations,
  including colored sugar

UTENSILS
baking sheets lined with aluminum foil,
a rolling pin, a table knife, waxed paper,
a flower-shaped cookie cutter,
a lifter, a cooling rack

1 Preheat the oven to 180°C (350°F).

2 Place your dough on a baking
sheet, then pat it and roll it out
with the rolling pin until it is a little
more than 0.5 cm (¼ in.) thick. Use
the table knife to cut out a large ring
33 cm (13 in.) in diameter (or as large
as will fit on the baking sheet) and
6 cm (2 ¼ in.) wide.

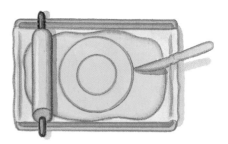

3 Place the remaining dough on a
piece of waxed paper and roll it
out until it is a little more than 0.5 cm
(¼ in.) thick. Use the cookie cutter to
cut out about 15 flowers. With the table
knife, cut out about 10 leaves. Carefully
transfer all the flowers and leaves to
another baking sheet. Sprinkle them
with colored sugar, if you like.

4 Bake the ring and the flower pieces for 12 to 15 minutes, or until golden brown. The ring will take longer to bake than the flowers. Remove all the pieces from the oven. Let the ring cool completely on the baking sheet. If you try to move it before it is completely cool, it may break. When the flowers and leaves have cooled for about 2 minutes, use the lifter to transfer them to the cooling rack.

5 When all the pieces are cool, use the table knife to spread icing on the backs of the flowers and leaves, then glue them onto the ring. (If no one will be eating the wreath, you can use white glue.) Attach any other decorations you wish.

OTHER IDEAS

• To hang the wreath, glue the cookie ring to a ring of heavy cardboard and loop ribbon around it.

• Use cookie cutters shaped like pumpkins, ghosts and witches to make a Halloween wreath.

• Make the wreath using two kinds of cookie dough to make different-colored decorations.

Cookie art

This picture is good enough to eat.

YOU WILL NEED

- 1 recipe of gingerbread cookie dough (page 34)
- 1 recipe of icing (page 38)
- cookie decorations

UTENSILS
2 baking sheets lined with aluminum foil,
a rolling pin, waxed paper,
cookie cutters, a lifter, a cooling rack,
a small, heavy plastic bag, scissors

1 Preheat the oven to 180°C (350°F).

2 Place a little less than half the dough on a baking sheet, then pat it and roll it out with the rolling pin until it is a little more than 0.5 cm (¼ in.) thick. This will be the base for your picture.

3 Place the remaining dough on a piece of waxed paper and roll it out until it is a little more than 0.5 cm (¼ in.) thick. Use the cookie cutters to cut out shapes for your picture. Carefully transfer the cookies to a baking sheet.

4 Bake the cookies and base for 12 to 15 minutes, or until the dough is no longer soft. The base will take longer to bake than the cookies. Remove all the pieces from the oven. Let the base cool completely on the baking sheet. If you try to move it before it is completely cool, it may break. When the cookies have cooled for about 2 minutes, use the lifter to transfer them to the cooling rack.

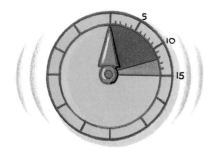

5 When all the pieces are cool, half fill the plastic bag with icing and snip off one corner. Pipe icing onto the backs of the cookies and stick them to the base. Use the icing to make designs and to glue other decorations in place.

OTHER IDEAS

• Make a birthday card for a friend by using alphabet cookie cutters to cut out letters and spell out your friend's name. Use other cookies, icing and candies to decorate your card.

• Make cards or pictures using sugar cookie dough (page 35) or oatmeal chocolate-chip cookie dough (page 33).

Candleholders

*Candleholders made of cookie dough?
You'll be surprised at how easy
they are to make.*

YOU WILL NEED

- 1 recipe of shortbread cookie dough
(page 36) (this will make 3 or 4
candleholders)
- 1 recipe of icing (page 38)
- cookie decorations, including colored
sugar or melted chocolate (page 38)

UTENSILS
waxed paper, a rolling pin,
a medium or large star-shaped cookie
cutter, a table knife, baking sheets lined
with aluminum foil, a lifter, a cooling rack,
a tall, thin candle for each candleholder

1 Preheat the oven to 150°C (300°F).

2 Place the dough on a piece of
waxed paper and roll it out with
the rolling pin until it is a little more
than 0.5 cm (¼ in.) thick.

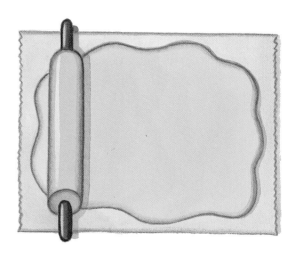

3 Use the cookie cutter to cut out
six stars for each candleholder
you want to make. In the center of each
star, use the table knife to cut out a
circle slightly larger than your candle
is around.

4 Carefully transfer the stars to the baking sheet. Sprinkle on colored sugar, if you like. Bake the stars for 15 to 17 minutes, or until golden brown. Remove from the oven. If the holes in the centers have filled in a little, carefully enlarge them with the table knife. The baking sheet will be hot, so ask an adult to help you. Let cool on the baking sheet for 2 minutes. Use the lifter to transfer the stars to the cooling rack to cool completely.

6 Decorate your candleholders, if you like.

OTHER IDEAS

• To make a birthday cake for a cookie lover, prepare oatmeal chocolate-chip cookie dough (page 33), roll it out until it is a little more than 0.5 cm (¼ in.) thick and cut out circles of various sizes. In the center of each circle, cut out a hole that's slightly larger than your candle. Bake the circles. When they are cool, stack them on top of each other, beginning with the largest and ending with the smallest. Put a candle in the hole and decorate your birthday cookie.

5 When the stars are cool, stack six on top of each other so that the holes in the middle are lined up and the tips of the stars aren't lined up. Repeat for each candleholder. Carefully put the candles in each holder.

Thanksgiving turkey

Here's a very special decoration for your Thanksgiving dinner table.

YOU WILL NEED

- 1 recipe of oatmeal chocolate-chip cookie dough (page 33)
- cookie decorations, including melted chocolate or icing (page 38)

UTENSILS

baking sheets lined with aluminum foil, a rolling pin, paper, scissors, a table knife, a small, heavy plastic bag

1 Preheat the oven to 180°C (350°F).

2 Place the dough on the baking sheet, then pat it and roll it out with the rolling pin until it is a little more than 0.5 cm (¼ in.) thick.

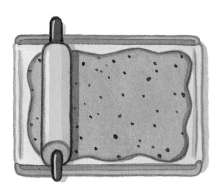

3 Enlarge the pattern pieces on page 39 (see page 5 for how to do this). You can make the pieces almost any size you like, as long as the largest piece will fit on a baking sheet. The sample shown here is twice the size of the pattern. Use the scissors to cut out the enlarged pattern pieces.

4 Using the paper pattern pieces as a guide, cut out the dough pieces with the table knife. Make sure the slit in each piece is at least as wide as the dough is thick.

6 When the pieces are cool, carefully peel the foil off the backs of the pieces. Decorate your turkey pieces any way you like. Half fill the plastic bag with melted chocolate or icing and snip off one corner. Pipe the chocolate or icing out of the bag and outline each of the pieces. Attach decorations.

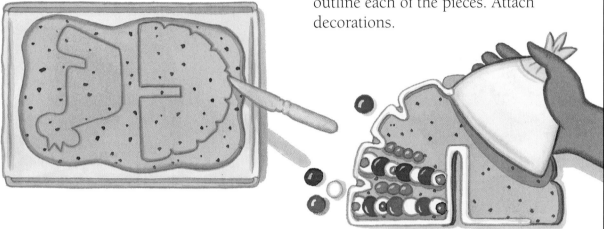

5 Bake the cookie pieces for 12 to 15 minutes, or until golden brown. Remove from the oven. If the slits have filled in, ask an adult to help you carefully enlarge them with the table knife. Let the pieces cool completely on the baking sheet.

7 Slide the turkey's tail into the body so that the turkey will stand. If you wish, glue the pieces in place using icing or melted chocolate.

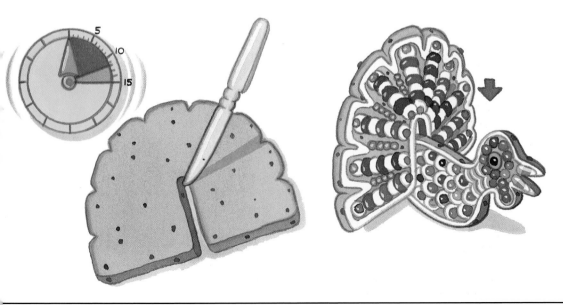

Cookie pets

Design a cookie to look like your pet — or any animal you wish.

YOU WILL NEED

- 1 recipe of sugar cookie dough (page 35)
- 1 recipe of icing (page 38)
- cookie decorations

UTENSILS
baking sheets lined with aluminum foil,
a rolling pin, a table knife,
waxed paper, a lifter, a cooling rack,
a small, heavy plastic bag, scissors

1 Preheat the oven to 180°C (350°F).

2 Place about half of the dough on a baking sheet, then pat it and roll it out with the rolling pin until it is a little more than 0.5 cm (¼ in.) thick. Cut out a base for your pet's face, using the table knife. It can be any size as long as it will fit on a baking sheet.

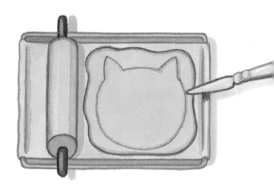

3 Place the remaining dough on a piece of waxed paper and roll it out until it is a little more than 0.5 cm (¼ in.) thick. Cut out whatever pieces you need to add to the face, such as eyes, cheeks, ears, a nose, hair and so on.

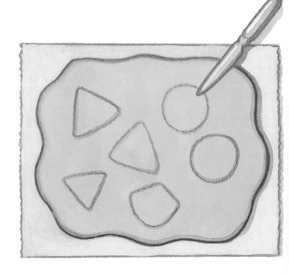

4 Carefully transfer the smaller pieces to baking sheets. Bake the face and face pieces for 12 to 15 minutes, or until golden brown. The face will take longer to bake than the smaller pieces. Remove from the oven. Let the face cool completely on the baking sheet. If you try to move it before it is completely cool, it may break. When the smaller pieces have cooled for about 2 minutes, use the lifter to transfer them to the cooling rack.

5 When all the pieces are cool, half fill the plastic bag with icing and snip off one corner. Pipe icing onto the backs of the small pieces and stick them to the face. You can also use the icing to make designs on the face and to glue other decorations in place. Shoestring licorice makes great whiskers or hair, and gumdrops make good noses.

OTHER IDEAS

• Make other animal faces or people faces. The faces can also be made from oatmeal chocolate-chip cookie dough (page 33).

• To make tusks or horns that stand up, roll and shape small cones of cookie dough. When baking the cones, stand them up on the baking sheet.

Cookie garden

*Make a flower garden
to decorate your table or create
a flower for each person.*

YOU WILL NEED

- 1 recipe of shortbread cookie dough
  (page 36) (this will make about
  12 finished flowers)
- cookie decorations, including melted
  chocolate and icing (page 38)

UTENSILS
waxed paper, a rolling pin, paper,
scissors, a table knife,
baking sheets lined with aluminum foil,
a lifter, a cooling rack,
a small, heavy plastic bag

1 Preheat the oven to 150°C (300°F).

2 Place the dough on a piece of
waxed paper and roll it out with
the rolling pin until it is a little more
than 0.5 cm (¼ in.) thick.

3 Trace the pattern piece on the next
page twice onto a piece of paper.
Cut out the two pieces as indicated on
the pattern. Use them as a guide to cut
out two pieces of dough for each flower.
Make sure the slits are at least as wide
as the dough is thick.

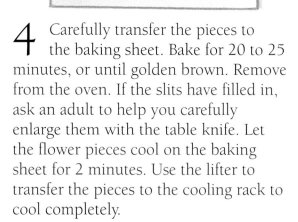

4 Carefully transfer the pieces to
the baking sheet. Bake for 20 to 25
minutes, or until golden brown. Remove
from the oven. If the slits have filled in,
ask an adult to help you carefully
enlarge them with the table knife. Let
the flower pieces cool on the baking
sheet for 2 minutes. Use the lifter to
transfer the pieces to the cooling rack to
cool completely.

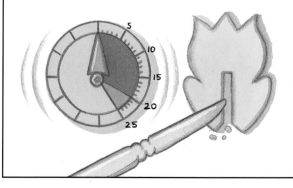

5 When the flower pieces are cool, take one with a top slit and one with a bottom slit and carefully slide them into each other as shown. Don't force them or they may break. If necessary, carefully cut or scrape the slit to make it a little wider.

6 Decorate your flowers any way you like. Fill the plastic bag with the icing or melted chocolate, snip off one corner and pipe designs on your flowers. Use the icing or chocolate as glue to attach decorations, if you wish.

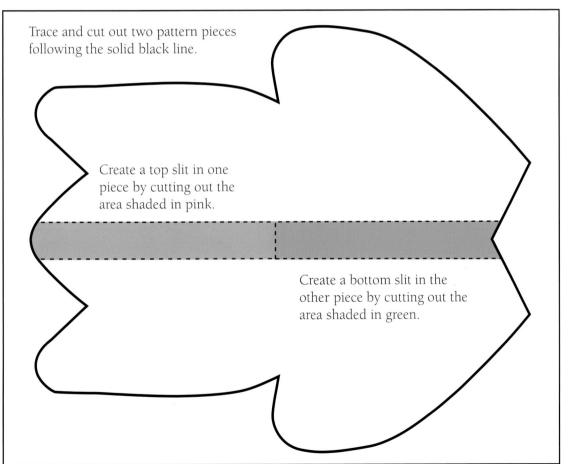

Trace and cut out two pattern pieces following the solid black line.

Create a top slit in one piece by cutting out the area shaded in pink.

Create a bottom slit in the other piece by cutting out the area shaded in green.

Star lantern

This lantern looks great when you light a candle in the center of it.

YOU WILL NEED

• 1 recipe of gingerbread cookie dough (page 34) (this will make 2 to 3 lanterns)

• 1 recipe of icing (page 38)

• cookie decorations (optional)

UTENSILS
waxed paper, a rolling pin, a table knife,
a star-shaped cookie cutter about
5 cm (2 in.) across at its widest point,
a large drinking straw,
a baking sheet lined with aluminum foil,
a lifter, a cooling rack,
a small, heavy plastic bag,
scissors, a short candle for each lantern

1 Preheat the oven to 180°C (350°F).

2 Place the dough on a piece of waxed paper and roll it out with the rolling pin until it is a little more than 0.5 cm (¼ in.) thick.

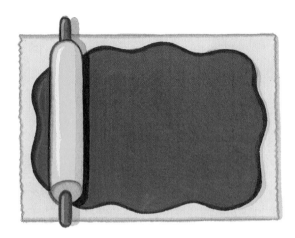

3 For each lantern, use the table knife to cut out a circle of dough about 12 cm (4 ¾ in.) across for a base. Use the cookie cutter to cut out five stars. With the straw, poke a few holes in each star.

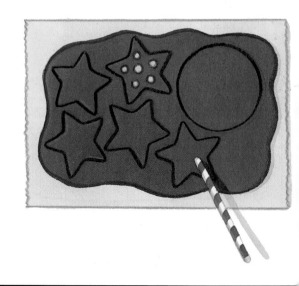

4 Carefully transfer the pieces to the baking sheet. Bake them for 12 to 15 minutes, or until the dough is no longer soft. Remove from the oven and let cool on the baking sheet for 2 minutes. Use the lifter to transfer the pieces to a cooling rack to cool completely.

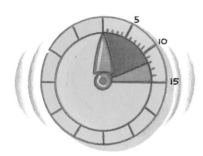

5 When the pieces are cool, half fill the plastic bag with icing and snip off one corner. Stand a star near the edge of the round base and use the icing to attach the star to the base. Stand another star beside the first one and attach it to the base and to the first star. Repeat until you've attached all the stars to the base. You may want to make the lantern in a small cookie tin and use crumpled aluminum foil to hold the pieces together while the icing hardens.

6 Decorate your lantern, if you like. Use the icing to attach candies and other decorations to the cookies. Place the candle in the center of the lantern.

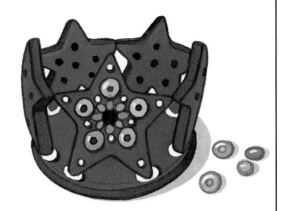

OTHER IDEAS

• Use flower-shaped cookie cutters.

• For a long-lasting lantern, use cinnamon applesauce cookie dough (page 37). Do not sprinkle on extra flour when rolling out this dough.

• Instead of a candle, place a vase of flowers in the middle of the ring of cookies.

Jack-o'-lantern

*This Halloween treat's
not scary — it's delicious.*

YOU WILL NEED

- 1 recipe of oatmeal chocolate-chip cookie dough (page 33) (this is enough for 2 jack-o'-lanterns)

- cookie decorations, including icing (page 38)

UTENSILS

a medium-sized metal bowl that is ovenproof, aluminum foil, a table knife, a small, heavy plastic bag, scissors

1 Preheat the oven to 180°C (350°F).

2 Line the inside of the bowl with aluminum foil. Fold any extra aluminum foil over the edges. Cover the inside of the bowl with a layer of dough a little more than 0.5 cm (¼ in.) thick. Working from the bottom of the bowl, pat the dough in place. Smooth the top edge of the dough with the table knife and your fingers.

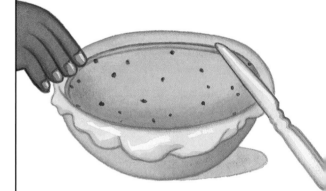

3 Using the table knife, cut out a jack-o'-lantern face from the dough.

4 Bake the dough in the bowl for 15 to 20 minutes, or until golden brown. If the edges brown too quickly, cover them with foil. Remove from the oven. Recut any bits of the face that have filled in — the bowl will be very hot, so ask an adult to help you. Leave the jack-o'-lantern in the bowl to cool completely.

6 Half fill the plastic bag with icing and snip off one corner. Pipe designs onto the jack-o'-lantern face or use the icing to glue decorations in place.

5 When cool, gently remove the jack-o'-lantern from the bowl, turn it over and peel off the aluminum foil.

OTHER IDEAS

• Make a cookie bowl to hold candies, brownies or even more cookies. If you like, decorate the outside and scallop the edge of the bowl.

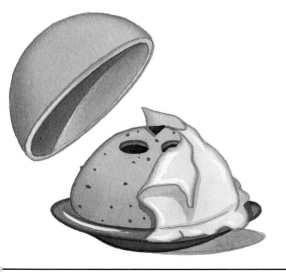

Scented decorations

These decorations aren't for eating, but they smell as good as they look.

YOU WILL NEED

• 1 recipe of cinnamon applesauce cookie dough (page 37) (this will make about 16 decorations)

UTENSILS

waxed paper, a rolling pin,
a star-shaped cookie cutter,
a large drinking straw,
a baking sheet lined with aluminum foil,
a lifter, a cooling rack, ribbon or twine

1 Preheat the oven to 110°C (225°F).

2 Place the dough on a large piece of waxed paper. Don't sprinkle flour on the waxed paper or rolling pin because the flour won't blend into this dough and will show. Pat the dough flat with your hands until it is about 1 cm (½ in.) thick, then use a clean rolling pin to roll out the dough until it is 0.5 cm (¼ in.) thick.

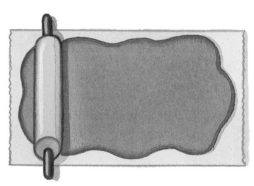

3 Cut out dough stars with the cookie cutter. Use the straw to make a hole near the top of each star as shown.

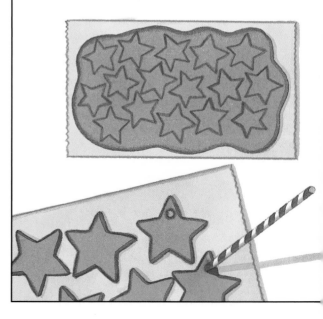

4 Carefully transfer the stars to the baking sheet and bake for 2 hours.

5 Remove the stars from the oven and let cool for 2 minutes. Use the lifter to transfer the stars to the cooling rack to cool completely.

6 When the stars are cool, thread a piece of ribbon, twine or lacing through the hole and tie the ends together to form a loop for hanging your decorations.

OTHER IDEAS

• You can make these decorations without using the oven. Place the stars on a drying or cooling rack and leave them for 2 days. If you don't have a rack, place the stars on a baking sheet or other flat surface and turn the stars at least twice a day. The finished decorations will be much lighter-colored than the baked decorations.

• Use different cookie cutters to make the decorations. Simple, large shapes work best with this dough. Or cut out your own shapes using a table knife.

• Make patterns in the cookies by using the straw to punch holes. Or use utensils such as knives and forks to make other designs.

• Cut out a variety of shapes and string them together.

Cookie castle

YOU WILL NEED

• 2 recipes of gingerbread cookie dough (page 34) (make the batches separately)

• 1 package clear, colored hard candy (such as Life Savers candy)

• 4 pointed ice-cream cones

• 4 straight pretzels

• cookie decorations, including fruit leather, shoestring licorice

• 2 recipes of icing (page 38)

UTENSILS

2 or more baking sheets lined with aluminum foil, a rolling pin, paper, a dull pencil, scissors, a table knife, a large drinking straw, a lifter, a cooling rack, piece of heavy cardboard at least 40 cm x 40 cm (16 in. x 16 in.), aluminum foil, a ruler, a small, heavy plastic bag, 8 large cans

1 Preheat the oven to 180°C (350°F).

2 Enlarge the pattern piece on page 40 (see page 5 for how to do this). You can enlarge the pattern piece as much as you wish, as long as it will fit on a cookie sheet. With the scissors, cut out the enlarged pattern piece.

3 Place half the dough from one cookie recipe on a baking sheet, then pat it and roll it out with the rolling pin until it is a little more than 0.5 cm (¼ in.) thick.

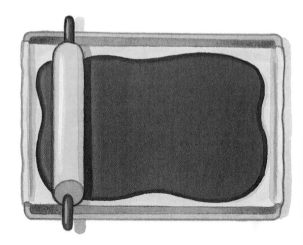

4 Using the pattern piece as a guide, cut out one piece of dough with the table knife. Cut carefully and accurately so that your pieces will fit together properly. Repeat steps 3 and 4 until you have cut out four identical pieces. These will be the walls of your castle.

6 Make the front of the castle by cutting out 4 windows and a drawbridge from one of the walls. Place the drawbridge on a baking sheet. Use the straw to poke two holes as shown in the drawbridge and two holes in the castle's front wall.

7 Group the hard candies by color so that all the red candies are together, all the greens are together and so on. Crush each group into small pieces. Bake the front wall of the castle for about 10 minutes. Ask an adult to help you remove the front wall from the oven and sprinkle a different color of crushed candy into each window hole. Return the front wall to the oven and bake for about another 5 minutes.

5 From the remaining dough, cut out four squares each measuring 5 cm x 5 cm (2 in. x 2 in.). Place them on a baking sheet. These pieces will be the bases for the turrets.

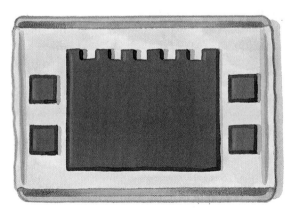

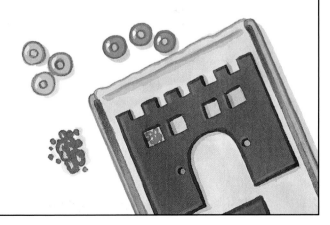

8 Bake the other cookie pieces for 12 to 15 minutes, or until the dough is no longer soft. The castle walls will take longer to bake than the small pieces. Be sure the walls are completely baked or they won't stand up well. Remove from the oven. After 2 minutes, use the lifter to transfer the smaller pieces to the cooling rack. Let the large pieces cool completely on the baking sheets.

9 Cover the board or piece of cardboard with aluminum foil. Measure the length of one of the walls of the castle (it may have expanded during the baking). Use the dull pencil to mark a square with sides of this length toward one end of the board. This is where you will build your castle.

10 When all the pieces are cool, half fill the plastic bag with icing and snip off one corner. Pipe a line of icing along one of the lines you marked on the board. Stand up one of the castle walls on this line, good side facing out. (A helper will make assembling the castle easier.) Place a can on either side of this wall to support it.

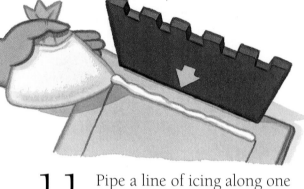

11 Pipe a line of icing along one edge of the wall and along the adjoining line on your board. Pipe icing along the edge of a second wall and press it firmly against the first wall. Have a helper hold it in place while you set cans on either side to support it. Pipe more icing inside the castle along the joint or along the base.

12 Continue adding walls until all four are standing. Leave the cans in place until the icing is hard.

13 To make a turret, gently poke a pretzel through the tip of an ice-cream cone. Glue the pretzel in place with icing. If you like, cut a flag out of fruit leather and use icing to glue it to the pretzel. Pipe icing around the opening of the cone and glue it to one of the gingerbread squares. Repeat for all four turrets and set them aside to harden.

14 Attach the turrets to each corner of the castle by piping icing onto the corners. Stand a turret on each corner and let the icing harden.

15 To attach the drawbridge, thread a piece of shoestring licorice through each hole in the drawbridge and through the matching hole in the castle wall. Tie a knot in each end.

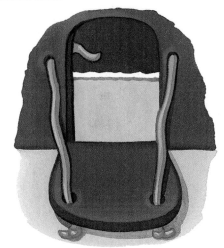

16 Add other decorations to your castle. Use the icing as glue to attach candies. Be sure to decorate the board around the castle. Use colored paper to add a moat or grass and sprinkle it with coconut "snow" if you like. Spearmint leaves make great bushes, and small bow-shaped pretzels make a good fence. You can even add gingerbread knights.

RECIPES

These cookie recipes not only make great projects — they also make great cookies.

ABBREVIATIONS

The following abbreviations have been used in the recipes:

mL = milliliter

c. = cup

tsp. = teaspoon

MEASURING INGREDIENTS

Both the metric and imperial systems of measurement are used in this book. The systems vary a little, so choose one system and use it for all of your measuring.

Dry ingredients and wet ingredients require different measuring cups. A dry measuring cup is flat across the top so you can level off the dry ingredients with a knife for a really accurate measure. A wet measuring cup has a spout to make pouring easier. Be sure to match your ingredients with the correct type of measuring cup.

Oatmeal chocolate-chip cookies

*Oatmeal and chocolate are
a delicious combination.*

YOU WILL NEED

250 mL	vegetable shortening, at room temperature	1 c.
250 mL	brown sugar, lightly packed	1 c.
250 mL	white sugar	1 c.
2	eggs	
5 mL	vanilla	1 tsp.
375 mL	all-purpose flour	1 ½ c.
5 mL	baking soda	1 tsp.
2 mL	salt	½ tsp.
925 mL	quick oatmeal	3 ¾ c.
125 mL	chocolate chips	½ c.

UTENSILS
measuring cups and spoons,
a large mixing bowl, a wooden spoon

1 In the mixing bowl, use the wooden spoon to cream together the shortening, brown sugar and white sugar.

2 Add the eggs and vanilla and beat well.

3 Mix the flour, baking soda and salt into the batter.

4 Add the oatmeal and blend in. Stir in the chocolate chips.

5 Use the dough to create one of the projects in this book. Or drop the dough in small mounds onto baking sheets lined with aluminum foil and bake at 180°C (350°F) for 10 to 12 minutes. Remove from the oven and let cool on the baking sheet for 2 minutes. Use a lifter to transfer the cookies to a cooling rack to cool completely. Makes about 6 dozen cookies.

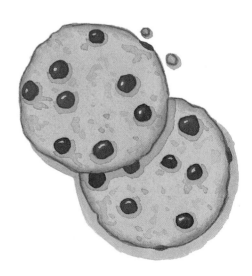

Gingerbread cookies

This recipe is especially good for making ornaments and gingerbread houses.

YOU WILL NEED

125 mL	margarine, at room temperature	½ c.
125 mL	brown sugar, lightly packed	½ c.
125 mL	cooking molasses	½ c.
75 mL	warm water	⅓ c.
875 mL	all-purpose flour	3½ c.
5 mL	baking soda	1 tsp.
5 mL	ground cinnamon	1 tsp.
5 mL	ground ginger	1 tsp.
2 mL	salt	½ tsp.

UTENSILS
measuring cups and spoons,
a large mixing bowl, a wooden spoon,
waxed paper

1 In the mixing bowl, use the wooden spoon to cream together the margarine and sugar.

2 Add the molasses and blend well. Mix in the water.

3 Add the flour, baking soda, cinnamon, ginger and salt and mix well.

4 Wrap the dough in waxed paper and chill for at least 1 hour.

5 Use the dough to create one of the projects in this book. Or place the dough on a piece of waxed paper and roll it out with the rolling pin until it is a little more than 0.5 cm (¼ in.) thick. Use cookie cutters to cut out shapes from the dough and place them on baking sheets lined with aluminum foil. Bake the cookies at 180°C (350°F) for 10 to 12 minutes or until golden brown. Remove from the oven and let cool on the baking sheet for 2 minutes. Use a lifter to transfer the cookies to a cooling rack to cool completely. Makes about 5 dozen cookies.

Sugar cookies

*Decorate these cookies with icing
or candies if you like.*

YOU WILL NEED

375 mL	butter, at room temperature	1 ½ c.
250 mL	white sugar	1 c.
125 mL	brown sugar, lightly packed	½ c.
2	eggs	
10 mL	vanilla	2 tsp.
1050 mL	all-purpose flour	4 ¼ c.
7 mL	baking powder	1 ½ tsp.
2 mL	salt	½ tsp.

UTENSILS
measuring cups and spoons,
a large mixing bowl, a wooden spoon

1 In the mixing bowl, use the wooden spoon to cream together the butter, white sugar and brown sugar.

2 Add the eggs and vanilla and mix well.

3 Add the flour, baking powder and salt and blend in.

4 Use the dough to create one of the crafts in this book. Or place the dough on a piece of waxed paper and roll it out with the rolling pin until it is a little more than 0.5 cm (¼ in.) thick. Use cookie cutters to cut out shapes from the dough and place them on baking sheets lined with aluminum foil. Bake the cookies at 180°C (350°F) for 10 to 12 minutes or until golden brown. Remove from the oven and let cool on the baking sheet for 2 minutes. Use a lifter to transfer the cookies to a cooling rack to cool completely. Makes about 5 dozen cookies.

Shortbread cookies

It's hard to believe these delicious cookies contain only three ingredients.

YOU WILL NEED

500 mL	butter, at room temperature	2 c.
250 mL	brown sugar, lightly packed	1 c.
1050 mL	all-purpose flour	4¼ c.

UTENSILS
measuring cups, a large mixing bowl, a wooden spoon

1 In the mixing bowl, use the wooden spoon to cream together the butter and brown sugar. If you like, wash your hands and use them to combine the butter and sugar. (Take off any rings first!)

2 Add the flour and mix in thoroughly — again, use your hands if you like.

3 Use the dough to create one of the crafts in this book. Or drop dough by the teaspoon onto baking sheets lined with aluminum foil and bake at 150°C (300°F) for 12 to 15 minutes or until just cooked. The cookies should still be very pale. Remove from the oven and let cool on the baking sheet for 2 minutes. Use a lifter to transfer the cookies to a cooling rack to cool completely. Makes about 5 dozen cookies.

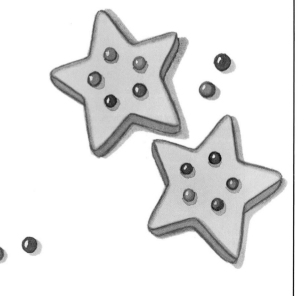

Cinnamon applesauce dough

You can't eat this dough, but it makes wonderfully scented decorations.

YOU WILL NEED

125 mL	cinnamon	½ c.
125 mL	all-purpose flour	½ c.
2 mL	salt	½ tsp.
250 mL	smooth applesauce (store-bought works best)	1 c.

UTENSILS

measuring cups and spoons, a large mixing bowl, a wooden spoon

1 In the mixing bowl, use the wooden spoon to combine the cinnamon, flour and salt.

2 Add the applesauce and blend well.

3 Use the dough to create one of the projects in this book. Or place the dough on a large piece of waxed paper. Don't sprinkle flour on the waxed paper or rolling pin because the flour won't blend into this dough and will show. Instead, pat the dough flat with your hands until it is abut 1 cm (½ in.) thick, then use a clean rolling pin to roll out the dough until it is 0.5 cm (¼ in.) thick. Use cookie cutters to cut out shapes from the dough and place them on baking sheets lined with aluminum foil. Bake the shapes at 110°C (225°F) for 2 hours. Remove from the oven and let cool on the baking sheet for 2 minutes. Use the lifter to transfer the shapes to a cooling rack to cool completely.

Icing

This icing dries very hard so it's great for gluing cookies together or for attaching candies to cookies.

YOU WILL NEED

500 mL	icing sugar	2 c.
1	egg white	
1 mL	cream of tartar	¼ tsp.
7 mL	warm water	1½ tsp.
	food coloring (optional)	

UTENSILS
measuring cups and spoons,
a mixing bowl, hand or electric mixer

1 In the mixing bowl, combine the icing sugar, egg white, cream of tartar and water. Beat for 8 to 10 minutes, or until the icing is stiff. If you are using an electric mixer, set it at high speed. If the icing is too thick, add a little more water.

2 You can add food coloring to the icing if you wish. Add the coloring a drop at a time until the icing is the color that you want. The icing will keep in a covered container in your refrigerator for about two weeks. Mix well before using and add a little more water if necessary.

Melted chocolate

Use melted chocolate chips or bars of semisweet or milk chocolate as "glue" to attach your cookie pieces together. (If you cut up the bars, the chocolate will melt faster.) You'll need about 50 mL (¼ c.) of melted chocolate for each craft.

Chocolate burns easily, so carefully melt it in a microwave or a double boiler. Ask an adult to help you. Heat the chocolate just enough to melt it, then let it cool slightly before you begin gluing with it. If the chocolate begins to harden before you are finished, melt it again.

Thanksgiving turkey pattern (for page 16)

These patterns are half size. To enlarge them, see the instructions on page 5.

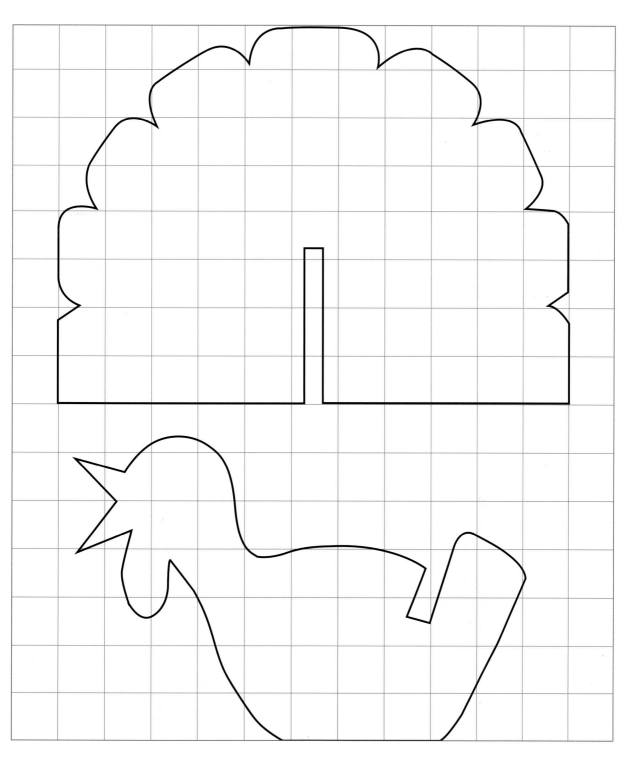

Castle pattern
(for page 28)

This pattern is half size. To enlarge it, see the instructions on page 5.

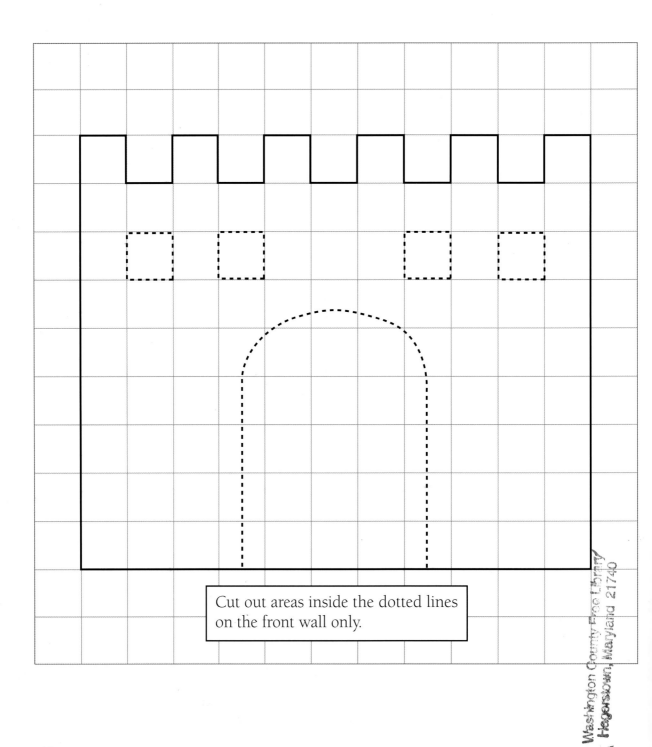

Cut out areas inside the dotted lines on the front wall only.